Curious Cooper
Have You Heard About Sharks?

written & illustrated by

Samantha Rezentes

Relevant
Publishers
LLC

SUTTON, ALASKA

Relevant Publishers LLC
P.O. Box 505
Sutton, AK 99674

LCCN: 2021936732

Publisher's Cataloging-In-Publication Data

Names: Rezentes, Samantha, author. | Rezentes, Samantha, illustrator.
Title: Curious Cooper Have You Heard About Sharks? / written by Samantha Rezentes ; illustrated by Samantha Rezentes.
Description: Sutton, Alaska : Relevant Publishers, LLC, [2021] | 0.8 Flesch-Kincaid. | Interest age level: 000-007.| Summary: "Curious Cooper and Remi go diving to learn more about sharks. A variety of sharks in their habitats are explored through rhymes and entertaining illustrations."--Provided by publisher.

Identifiers: LCCN: 2021936726 | ISBN 9781953263025 (paperback) | ISBN 9781953263032 (ebook)
Subjects: LCSH Sharks--Juvenile literature. | Marine animals--Juvenile literature. | CYAC Sharks. | Marine animals. | BISAC JUVENILE NONFICTION / Animals / Marine Life | JUVENILE NONFICTION / Readers / Beginner | JUVENILE NONFICTION / Science & Nature / General | JUVENILE NONFICTION / Science & Nature / Zoology
Classification: LCC QL638.9 .R49 Cur 2021 | DDC 597/.31--dc23

Printed in the United States of America

DEDICATION

For the real Cooper and Remi
&
all the curious little ones
with love.

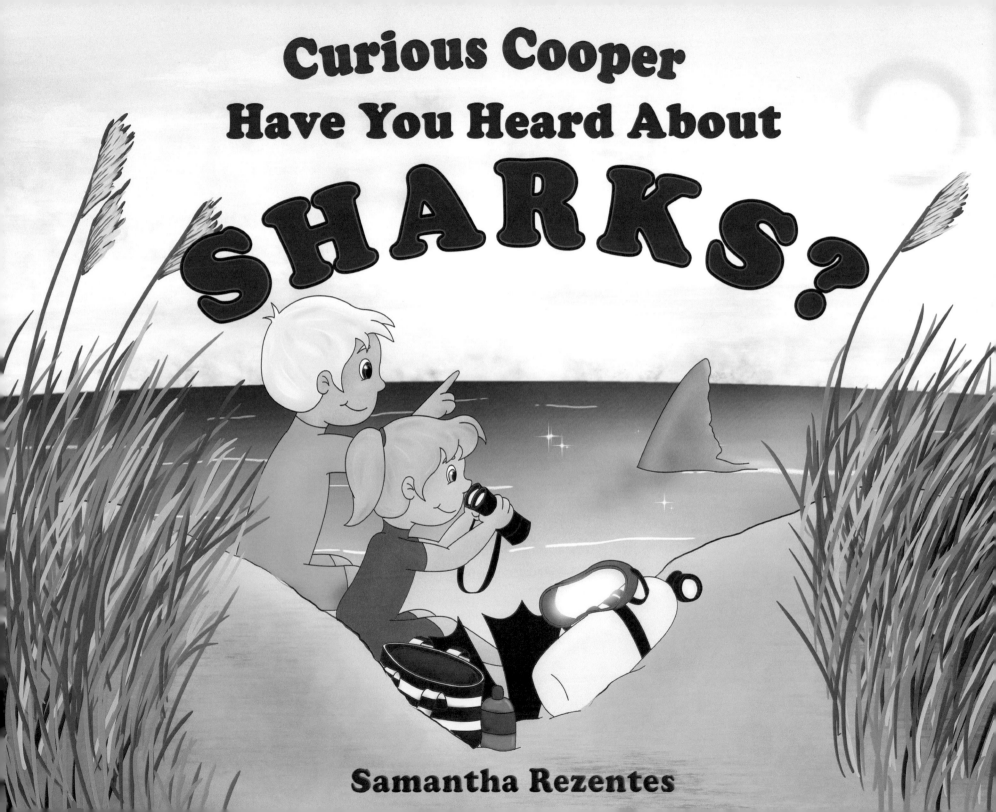

Cooper and Remi wave "Hello!" Come on! It's time to play!
Won't you join us on our dive? We'll meet some sharks today!

Cooper sees a zebra shark. Where are all his stripes?
The zebra shark grew out of them. Now spots are what he likes!

Remi sees a big bull shark making up his mind.
Should he swim up the river, or out into the tide?

How about the horn shark, with his tiny purple teeth?
The purple comes from urchins that the horn shark loves to eat!

Cooper sees a great white shark swimming through the sea.
He travels all the oceans wide, roaming far and free!

Remi sees a mako shark. Look how fast he swims!
Dolphins may be quick. But the mako always wins!

Do you see the reef sharks, all black, white and grey?
Look! They're joining Coop and Remi for sushi here today!

Can you spot the angel sharks hiding in the sand?
How many are lying there? Try counting on your hand!

Cooper sees a Greenland shark who travels very slow.
He doesn't care what time it is. He's never on the go.

Remi sees a nurse shark family lying in their beds.
Did you know they snuggle up when they lay down their heads?

Do you see that tiger shark? He won't turn up his snout.
When this shark is hungry, he'll eat anything about!

How about those bonnetheads, cheering for their troop?
They don't like to be alone. They like to swim in groups!

Cooper sees a basking shark with his big mouth open wide.
He scoops up tiny plankton from the sea as he goes by!

All the sharks we've met just now have vital roles to play!
Each of us must care for them so they don't go away!

Well, it was fun to meet the sharks. Now it's time to go.
We hope you'll come with us again, as we find new things to know!

THE END

Check out our other books at

www.relevantpublishers.com

CPSIA information can be obtained
at www.ICGtesting.com
Printed in the USA
BVRC102015251121
622522BV00003B/42